Special Educational Needs:

Getting Started With Statements

Advice on how to start writing your child's application for statutory assessment and beyond

by

Tania Tirraoro

the creator of

www.specialneedsjungle.co.uk

Published by FeedARead.com Publishing –
Arts Council funded

A CIP catalogue record for this title is available from the British Library.

Contents

Foreword by Maria Hutchings

It was in February 2005 that I challenged Tony Blair, then Prime Minister, on live television, over the poor provision of services for special needs children and their families.

There was nothing particularly special about me; it was my son who was special.

John Paul was diagnosed with autism, severe learning disabilities and severe, specific language disorder when he was three and a half. He was, and still is, hugely vulnerable and deserves all the help he can get. As a society I strongly feel that we must be judged on how we look after people just like him.

But knowing how to get help, who to speak to and where to go (as well as dealing with the challenge of your child's condition) is all too often confusing, stressful and downright torture.

I only wish that I when I was going through the statementing process striving to get John Paul the right education, speech therapy and respite for the family that I had read this book.

Being the mother of two children on the autistic spectrum, Tania has a deep sense of empathy for what it feels like when you have to fight for everything to ensure your child's future. Tania captures that deep sense we all have as mothers and carers; to do the very best for our precious children.

But further still at the turn of every page Tania guides you through the processes that one has to go through to get results. This book is comprehensive, user-friendly and straight to the point. Navigating your way through the statementing process your case will not be won on emotion alone, but trying to understand the law and using it to win.

Parents know that they understand their children best and therefore it is essential that they equip themselves in the best possible way to fight their children's corner and here in the following pages Tania helps you do just that.

Maria Hutchings

October 2011

Introduction

First of all, let me state that this book is aimed at parents in the UK, but it also contains useful tips for any parent anywhere who is seeking access to special educational needs for their child.

This book complements my website, www.specialneedsjungle.co.uk. It contains some information already available there but the main aim of the book is to give you solid, successful examples of applications, showing you a logical and thorough way to set out your child's case.

Realising your child has special educational needs is stressful for any parent. Getting them the help they require can be a long, drawn-out, frustrating and expensive process. All too often, the school does not tell the parent that their child has needs that could best be met by statement-level help. They do not tell the parent that they, themselves can apply for a statutory assessment if the school doesn't want to, or offer information and advice on how to go about it.

If your child has severe physical needs, they will almost certainly have been statemented before or immediately after they began school. This book is primarily for parents setting out on the statementing journey whose children have a so-called "hidden" disability such as high-functioning ASD or dyslexia that is much more difficult to see, just by looking at the child. It's no walk in the park to go through this process and if you honestly think you may not have the skills yourself to work through it, I strongly urge you to seek assistance from one of the charities set up to help people through the process such as IPSEA or SOS!SEN. There are links at the end of the book or on the www.specialneedsjungle.co.uk website.

You should be convinced that your child has special educational needs that the school is not able to support. Your child may already be on School Action Plus with little sign of improvement, but even if he is only on School Action, it does not mean you cannot apply for a statutory assessment. It may be that the school hasn't recognised the full extent of your child's needs because a serious assessment is needed.

If your child is at an independent school or home-schooled, you are just as entitled to apply for a statutory assessment as a parent with a child at a state school. The SEN Code of Practice says that, the question to be answered when making a decision to assess is whether there is convincing evidence that, in spite of efforts made by the school, along with the help of external specialists, taking relevant and purposeful action to meet the child's learning difficulties, those difficulties remain or have not been remedied sufficiently.

When schools are dealing with the complex needs of a child with a "hidden disability" such as Asperger Syndrome, or another social or communication-related disorder it is often extremely difficult for them to provide the right support because they do not have the day-to-day expertise needed.

One child I know had been diagnosed with Asperger Syndrome and was a gifted reader but had extreme difficulty with the process of writing. He had a unique thinking style but had also been judged to be extremely bright. The school's solution was to put him in the remedial English class with the children who could neither read nor write. He became distressed when he had to go to the class and had to be "dragged" by his classmates. This is despite the school having recommendations given to them by the LEA Educational Psychologist and an ASD Outreach worker on how best to help him. The school simply did not have the expertise to carry out the recommendations

Often, children like these can achieve well in some areas and parents are told, erroneously, that their children will never get a statement because they are not far enough behind. I have often heard of parents being told that their child needs to be "three years behind" to be assessed. This is not the case when the causes of the SEN are for example, Autistic Spectrum Disorders or Behavioural, Emotional or Social or other complex needs. This book will be particularly useful for children such as these.

The fact is, for many high-functioning Autistic Spectrum Disorder (ASD) children or those with dyslexia, dyspraxia or dyscalculia, a mainstream school often does not have the expertise or the resources needed to provide an "adequate" education because these children need a different style of teaching.

LEAs are also focused on so-called "inclusion" but miss the point that the ultimate goal is to enable children to be included in society as an adult. Making them all dance to the same tune in a test-driven, national curriculum based, mainstream education system will turn mainstream children into successful mainstream adults, but those "square peg" children who do not fit into the "round hole" of the state system may end up never reaching their potential.

If you have already put your child in a private specialist school and are paying the fees yourself, you may think they have improved so much that they will not get a statement. It may be more difficult, but it is not an impossible task. If your child has only improved because they were in a specialist environment, then that fact should be weighed against how they would be doing and coping if they were in mainstream. However, it will make your argument more complex so the sooner you apply the better.

What is Statementing?

A statement is a legally enforceable document listing your child's special educational needs and how they will be provided for by your local education authority (LEA).

A statutory assessment is carried out to determine what those needs are and you are a vital part of that process. It is up to you to make sure that all the evidence – that is, reports, letters, IEPs, school reports, assessments, that have been done into your child's issues are presented to the special educational needs panel. Don't rely on anyone else to do it for you.

The SEN Code of Practice says:

"In deciding whether to make a Statutory Assessment, the critical question is whether there is convincing evidence that, despite the school, with the help of external specialists taking relevant and purposeful action to meet the child's learning difficulties, those difficulties remain or have not been sufficiently remedied and may require the Local Education Authority to determine the child's special educational provision."

The statement follows the successful completion of a statutory assessment, which aims to uncover all your child's special educational needs.

So, before you embark upon the process, you must have exhausted all the help the school can offer through its own resources. This usually means resources funded at School Action or School Action Plus level. There may have been input from an LEA Educational Psychologist or an Outreach worker or perhaps a Speech and Language Therapist. If these outside agencies have been consulted and have made recommendations and the school simply hasn't carried them out you need to ask them why. If they don't have the resources to carry our recommendations, try to get them to say this in writing.

Once you have decided to go ahead and apply for an assessment for your child, I would recommend that you do not rush into contacting your LEA until you have gathered together your evidence or you will be putting undue pressure on yourself.

This is because once you write to the LEA they have six weeks to respond as to whether you will get your requested assessment. They need some evidence to go on and will be asking your child's school for IEPs, end of year reports and opinions. You will be asked for your parental input, usually on a form with headings and spaces. You can, of course, just fill in the form they send to you, attach any doctor's letters or private assessments and hope for the best.

I would urge you to be more thorough. This book will show you how.

~~~

You may be wondering what my qualifications are to write this guide. I am a parent who has been through the process twice and been successful on both occasions

Both my children have high-functioning Asperger Syndrome and associated co-morbidities such as dyspraxia, attention or hyperactivity issues. They are both in the gifted range for intelligence but their individual difficulties are very different from each other's.

They had/have complex needs that were very difficult for their state school to recognise, understand or remedy. As a regular parent-helper, I witnessed these difficulties for myself on many occasions but when I raised the possibility of seeking a statutory assessment, I was told that the chance of securing a statement would be very unlikely.

Undeterred, I studied the LEA's policies and the SEN Code of Practice. I gathered all the reports, IEPs and medical letters that proved my case and I carefully wrote long documents in support of my application. Initially both my children were turned down for assessment, but the LEA changed their minds before or just after I registered an appeal.

The LEA now funds them both to attend an independent specialist school and they are both progressing well. So, whatever you are told, if you are convinced that your child must be assessed to uncover the extent of their difficulties, stick to your guns.

I have since advised other parents on their applications, from a simple conversation to helping them draft their application. I am lucky; I have a journalistic background and had the skills to carry out an immense amount of research to ensure that I made the best application I could. I realised that there must be many parents in my position who do not have the skills I have and their children were just as in need of help as mine. So, I developed my SEN website and now am extending that to give you a step-by-step guide to making your application for assessment hard to ignore.

If, despite this, you are turned down at first, having followed these steps, you will be well prepared for an appeal with all your documents gathered and your parental submissions ready to be heard. In some cases, no matter how good your application, the LEA will turn you down first time in the hope that you will just go away. Lodging an appeal against them and showing just how serious you are is sometimes all that is needed for them to look at your case again.

I'm not a lawyer or a child development expert. This book is parent-to-parent, illustrating what has worked in real cases through extracts from example applications.

A green paper was launched in 2011 aimed at shaking up SEN delivery with a single assessment. Whatever changes and whenever the changes proposed become law, you will still need to be able to show that your child has sufficient special needs to attract the highest levels of support and this book can help. Do not wait for the new act, before you start the process. You child needs help as soon as you can get it.

Some LEAs are trialling the new proposals alongside the existing system, but you will still need to prepare your case carefully, however they change their systems. Although eventually there may be no more 'statements' you will still need to be able to make your case for that level of support and this book will show you how.

The SEN Code of Practice & SEN Law

The SEN Code of Practice is your friend. Download it or order a hard copy. Whatever you do, read it.

The SEN Code of Practice (2001) has four separate areas: Special Educational Need. They are: Cognition and Learning, Behavioural, Emotional and Social Development (BESD), Communication and Interaction and Sensory and/or Physical Needs. Your child does not need a deficit in all four areas to be considered in need of a statutory assessment.

For example, BESD becomes a learning disability when children have difficulties such as being withdrawn, being disruptive, hyperactivity, lack of concentration, immature social skills or other challenging behaviours. These difficulties can lead to an inability to manage school routines, relationships or learning techniques which can affect learning and progress. These can include Asperger's Syndrome, Dyspraxia or DCD, ADD, ADHD, Conduct Disorders, Semantic Pragmatic Disorders and so on.

Above all, it is UK education law and the SEN Code of Practice that count, not the LEA's own policies if they are in contradiction with them. Although the SEN Code of Practice is non-statutory, it is there as guidance. It is the Education Act 1996, the SEN Regulations and the Equalities Act 2010 which truly govern an appeal to the SEND Tribunal and a child's educational and disability rights.

The SEN Code of Practice is available free and you can download it from the Department for Education website. The Education Act (1996), The Education (Special Educational Needs) (England) (Consolidation) Regulations 2001and the Equalities Act (2010) are all also available online for you to read.

Getting Prepared

Applying for a statutory assessment and a statement is very stressful and time consuming. Consider the following:

1. Am I convinced that this is the only way my child will get the support they need?

Research your council's SEN policies to support your case. Read the SEN Code of Practice and use it. Make sure the school has tried everything within its resources to help your child and yet they haven't improved.

2. Do I have the support of friends and family to help me through it?

Having someone to talk to, will help you get through the process. If you're alone, try some of the parenting boards on the internet for support if you need it.

3. Do I have the funds to hire specialist help such as independent Educational Psychologist or an SEN lawyer if I need to?

You may not need to, but the question is worth asking in any case. You need to go into this process with your eyes open.

4. Do we have the backing of my child's paediatrician?

You will need reports from doctors to strengthen your case. Having said that, my son's doctor didn't think we'd get a statement which just made me more determined.

5. Do I have a good relationship with the school's SENCo (Special Needs Coordinator)?

If not, try to build one. They're often afraid to help too much so they don't get into trouble with the LEA but if you can get them on your side, they can help in all sorts of ways. Some are brilliant, some are useless. If you get one of the latter, your job will undoubtedly be more difficult, but don't let it get you down or put you off.

~~~

This book is not anti-LEA but LEAs have budgets to stick to and the power to decide where they will spend it. This site is to help parents get started on cutting their way through the special needs jungle from a parent's perspective, so they know what help is out there for them to get the education their child needs. It will also hopefully help you see that it is no good just filling in the form they send you with no evidence and crossing your fingers. It takes work and it takes time. When my spirits were flagging, I always reminded myself that I wasn't doing it for myself; I was doing it for my child.

Producing a well-researched application backed up by evidence, shows the LEA that you are one of those parents who are determined, serious and willing to put in the work to make sure their child gets what they need. All too often it is the parents who are less capable or less knowledgeable or simply just too exhausted who fail to secure the correct help for their children.

This is not a fair situation and is part of the reasoning behind this book. I hope that this will be inspiring to those who are setting out on this journey and will help them get started on the path to securing the best possible future for their son or daughter.

Statement Checklist

If you think your child's evident needs (evident to you, that is) will ensure that they will get the help they need, think again. Many parents go into applying for a statement without really knowing what it is or how difficult it can be to get one, so before you apply for a statutory assessment, read the tips below. The following notes are also available on my website www.specialneedsjungle.co.uk, so that you can print them off if you need to.

1. Find out how the school thinks your child is doing. First of all you should speak to your child's head teacher or the Special Educational Needs Coordinator, or SENCo. Find out what level of support they are already on, such as School Action or School Action Plus and for how long they have been on each level. Ask to see their Individual Educational Plan (IEP) and ask how it has been monitored and whether your child has achieved their targets. Get concrete evidence for whatever the IEP says has been achieved. Ask the SENCo if they could spare the time to make a list of all the educational/behavioural interventions used for your child and their results. This should give you an idea of exactly what your child is achieving and you should be able to compare it with the average expected level for a child of their age.

2. Gather together any reports or tests your child has ever had done. This means all their school reports and

exam results, any referrals they have had to Paediatricians, Occupational Therapists, Physiotherapists, Speech and Language Therapists, Educational Psychologists, etc. Make a file up if you haven't done so already and put the reports in chronological order. You are building up a paper profile of your child because you will need to prove that your child needs the help you say they do.

3. Find out what your child should be achieving. The LEA will argue that just because a child is achieving below average does not mean that they need a statement of Special Educational Needs. Children in each class will have a broad spectrum of achievement according to their individual potential. Harsh as it seems, some children will never be top of the class but that doesn't mean that they have SEN. So, how can you show that your child has a greater potential than their current achievements point to? The obvious way is to secure an Educational Psychology Assessment for them. Each LEA has its own Ed Psychs, although there is something of a shortage. Try to build up and maintain a positive relationship with your school's SENCo if possible and ask them to request an Educational Psychology evaluation for your child, and/or an assessment from the Learning and Language Team, if appropriate. If this happens, you can submit it with your application, making sure to quote from the parts that support your case. If an Ed Psych assessment is not forthcoming, you could consider a private assessment, usually at great expense, although these are often regarded with suspicion by the LEA that the report is biased towards the parents' views, even

though it almost certainly isn't.

4. If applicable, get a medical diagnosis for your child. Some people don't like labelling their child, which is fine unless you want to get the state to provide them with the help they need. If little Johnny is dyslexic, ASD, ADHD, dyscalculic or any other hidden disability, you need to be able to prove that this is not just your opinion, even if you are a doctor yourself. Take your child to your GP and ask for a referral to a paediatrician. A firm medical diagnosis is harder to ignore.

5. Do Your Research. Knowledge is power and in such a David v. Goliath match as the LEA vs. the parent is (though the fact that it's seen as adversarial is a scandal), this is even more important. The internet means this is not as difficult as it seems. Find out what your LEA's SEN policies are. You can find a lot of information on their websites. The government also has an SEN Code of Practice, which you can download in pdf format the Department for Education website.

6. Once you have the information you need, you need to know what to do with it. If your LEA has a document outlining its policies, read and analyse it. Make it work for you. Use its own policies to show that your child isn't getting what they should be. After all, if you can't prove this, you case will be considerably weaker. When you send in your submission, don't use their own form if you don't want to. Write as much as you can that is relevant to your case and provide reports to back them up. Refer to the reports in your document. Approach it like you are writing a report at work or at college. This may take many redrafts and a lot of time. You may feel

you need help and if so don't be afraid to ask (see 8.) Remember this is not for you; it's for your child.

7. Stay strong. There is no doubt that this process is stressful and often depressing and many parents give up along the way, which is what the LEA is hoping for. If your child has severe and visible needs, you are less likely to be reading this because those cases are self-evident and easier to prove, although this is not always true. It is where a child has a hidden disability that things get trickier. It is completely true that only the most determined will get what they want. You must look after your own physical and mental health in order to help your child. That means eating healthily, sleeping enough (not easy if your child is up a lot in the night), and just doing whatever works for you to keep you going. Remember you are your child's greatest asset and best advocate. Don't give up.

8. Get help. Not everyone is great at reading and analysing great tracts of text and complex documents. This is sometimes because the parents themselves have an ASD or are dyslexic; these conditions do, after all, have a genetic component. If this sounds like you, then ask a friend for support or approach some of the excellent charities that can help.

9. Most importantly, know your child. Only you know how they react in certain situations, what their triggers are, how a bad day at school affects them at home. This is important information for your application as it can be evidence of how an inappropriate educational setting is affecting their entire life and the rest of the family's life as well.

Where to start? – Parental views & evidence.

Parents have been turned down many times because of a lack of supporting evidence of their child's needs. This is partly the fault of some councils sending out the kind of form they do, with only a miniscule space for parents to state why they think their child should be assessed for a statement. Many parents think this is all they are allowed to submit.

The LEA wants to have your views of your child's needs but I would suggest that this is simply not enough to form a strong application. Views not backed up by evidence can easily be disregarded.

While it is necessary to include anecdotal evidence, it is just as important to be able to back up your opinions with reports that tell the same story— that your child has special educational needs that cannot be met within the normal school day or at School Action Plus.

Your school's SENCo will be asked for a submission as well, but do not rely on her to do your job for you. Often Special Needs Coordinators are not dedicated positions and you are trusting a harried, overworked teacher to be as well-versed in the SEN Code of Practice or even your LEA's SEN policies as perhaps they should be.

So, where to start? I would recommend that you begin your first draft—yes, you will need to do more than write it out once to get the best document—by simply telling your child's story. No one knows this better than you. I am going to pose a series of questions below that may jog your memory about things you had forgotten but may be extremely relevant to your case.

You will almost certainly find writing your story a deeply emotional experience. You may remember things that happened that you had not previously put into context. It is important that you start at the beginning, before the baby was born and work through your memories. It will remind you of remarks that others made to you about your child—such as comments made by pre-school or infant school teachers or even your health visitor. Get out your red book—your child's personal health record, look back through your photo albums and refresh your memory.

Consider:

- Did you have a difficult pregnancy or was it a traumatic birth for the baby?

- If you had experienced other pregnancies, did this pregnancy feel different in any way i.e. did the baby move more or were his movements not very vigorous?

- Was the baby pre-term or were there other complications that may have contributed to the learning difficulties he now has?

- What was he like as a baby? Happy, difficult to please?

- Did he seem as if he was always on the go and didn't sleep much?

- Was it difficult to establish feeding or was your baby

hungry all the time?

- Did your child have difficulty maintaining concentration or did he seem exceptionally focused on certain things/topics?

- How about eye contact? Did your child avoid eye contact completely, make fleeting eye contact or hold their eye contact so long that it felt a little bit unnerving.

- How did they get on at forming early relationships with peers? Were they invited for tea or to parties?

- Did your child seem different to other children of the same age?

- How did/does your child react to getting dressed or washed? Is he sensorily sensitive to having things put over his head or having his hair washed? How about teeth cleaning?

- At school was his progress even—could he for example read well but struggle with writing?

- Did he stare out of the window all the time?

- Was he unhappy? Was it difficult to get him to go to school?

- Could he sit in a lesson all day and produce nothing?

- Is he disruptive or always demanding attention from the teacher?

- Did he learn his numbers and letters at a regular pace?

- Can he tell the time on an analogue clock if he is of an age at which he should be able to do so?

- Has he had any medical problems that have affected his learning?

- Does he have a normal sleep pattern?

This is not an exhaustive list but it should help you start to make some notes and dig out any evidence you may have forgotten about. These are all issues to consider. Get out all the reports you have gathered and go through them carefully. Pick out the points that support your case. Make notes of them and refer to them in your application and add your own comments.

Providing evidence is crucial to supporting your case. If you haven't kept all your child's reports, IEPs, medical letters, don't despair. There will be copies held at the school and by the doctor. You have a right to this information under the Data Protection Act. Even so, it may be daunting to ask for copies, especially if your relationship with the school isn't good, but remember who it's for. It's not about you; it's about your child. Hold that mantra in your head and repeat it often, it will give you more courage than you imagine.

Example Applications

Everyone's application will be different, tailored to their own child, but often people don't know where to start.

As mentioned, the council will send you a form to fill in but the space for you to say why you think your child should be assessed for a statement is tiny. I suggest you use that space to write "Please see attached document entitled: "Parent's Report" This leaves you with the scary task of writing that report. Once you actually get started, it won't be so daunting.

Below are extracts from several cases made for children to be statutorily assessed that were ultimately successful. As you will see from the extracts, they are very detailed and are accompanied by evidence from schools, in the form of IEPs, end of year reports and letters. It also refers to evidence from an independent Educational Psychologist, his paediatrician and a doctor from CAMHS (Child and Mental Health Service) At the end of the actual documents there are lists of appendices (which are not included here as they contain confidential medical information). Each appendix is numbered and it corresponds to the numbering where it is quoted in the document so that the person reading the application can find the relevant appendix. The actual appendix item is also numbered accordingly.

Do not be put off by the detail that is specific to Child A. Some of it may be relevant to your child's difficulties, much of it may not be. It is intended to act as a springboard from which you can be inspired to write your own submission.

Evidence is vital is you are to support your case. After all, if you have no evidence, or fail to produce it when asking for an assessment, how can the LEA decide in your favour?

You are welcome to use anything from this document for your own needs, if the wording suits your own child. Bear in mind, this example was worked on over several drafts and may seem daunting but you will be surprised by how much you can write once you get started. If you really don't think you can manage, contact IPSEA, SEN!SOS or the NAS Advocacy Service (if your child has an ASD). There is also the local Parent Partnership, although the quality of this can vary. They should be able to help. You will surprise yourself with how much you can write. When you've done – READ IT THROUGH. Edit out anything that is irrelevant or unsupportive to the case. Check your spelling with a dictionary or a spellchecker if you've typed it. It doesn't need to be of PhD standard—it's your parental views after all. But the easier it is to understand, the better your chances will be.

~~~

EXAMPLE, CHILD A: Why we believe Child A should be Statutorily Assessed

EXTRACT 1:

❛   We are applying for a statutory assessment for our son, Child A, who has been diagnosed with Asperger's Syndrome with Hyperactivity. Child A was on School Action from his time at "School C Infant" until when we withdrew him from mainstream in Year Five at School 1 Junior.

First of all, we must begin by stating this case is not about pure academic underachievement. Child A is a bright and able boy but one whose social and communication difficulties are so underlying and pervasive that they affect his entire educational social and emotional experience of school. His problems sabotage his ability to make the most of his learning opportunities and they have been on-going since he was in pre-school, but because of his apparent academic abilities in comparison to other children, they have been over-looked or treated as naughtiness.

It is important for the purposes of this appeal that clause 7:39 of the Code of Practice is given due consideration:

".... academic attainment is not in itself sufficient for LEAs to conclude that a statutory assessment is or is not necessary."

NOTE: *The use of the SEN Code of Practice to support the application. This also shows the LEA that you know what you are talking about.*

The introduction continues:

EXTRACT 2:

' Autism, and in particular, Asperger's Syndrome, is a 'hidden disability' and the level of help people require is not always obvious to people with little knowledge of the condition and this includes many teachers. Due to their social and communication difficulties, the behaviour of someone with autism can also be easily misinterpreted and they may be mistakenly labelled as 'difficult' or uncooperative. This is very true of Child A's difficulties and if academic ability was the only measure of success in school then we would not be applying for an assessment. It is his ASD social and communication difficulties that put this present achievement and future potential at risk and affect the quality of his work on a daily basis, that we believe needs close investigation.

We cannot blame his mainstream schools entirely for this lack of understanding - it was not until he was assessed at School 2 and by an independent Educational Psychologist that we realised the extent of it ourselves, which is why we have not previously applied for an assessment.

Child A was on School Action for several years until we moved him to School 2. I believe his social issues should have meant he was on School Action+ but firstly, the surface of his problems had not been scratched and secondly, the school judged him on his academic ability in relation to other children, rather than on his own potential and shortcomings. Had they done this, it would have been clear that his social needs were in danger of damaging his academic progress and should have been more seriously addressed.

Therefore, I believe the fact that he was not on SA+ *must be discounted* as it stemmed from an inadequate understanding of his condition and not through a lack of need.

NOTE:

This was a key point in this particular case. It is important to leave no room for the LEA to interpret the case in any way other than the way you want them to. It also illustrates that a child does not HAVE to have been on School Action Plus – this child was receiving statement level help in all but name before the assessment was applied for.

EXTRACT 3:

❛ Ever since Child A was a baby, we always said, "He's not like other children", but if you had pressed us at the time, we would not have been able to tell you why. He did everything early – walking, talking, jigsaws, reading, writing – but always seemed to be in such a rush and it always seemed as if he was driven by a powerful motor. He would be difficult to control, refuse to share and would run around excessively, so much so that we stopped going to toddler group because he was a danger to other children.

Even at pre-school, it was noted that he was extremely stubborn, sensorily sensitive to his surroundings and overly clumsy – something of a bull in a china shop. He would fall over a lot and accidentally break things because he seemed to always be moving so fast without noticing his surroundings. He could not put a jumper with a smallish neck-hole over his head without a major screaming upset and we could not wash his hair without a tantrum and tears. When put in his room, (he had to be physically taken there because he would refuse to go) he would repeatedly kick at the door, scrawl his name on the walls and lash out at anyone who came near.

Since toddlerhood, Child A would fly into a rage if he didn't get what he wanted and it would be very difficult to placate him. This was not the usual 'terrible-twos' kind of tantrums that we would see in other children and as he grew older, he continued to have these long-lasting, deep sulks and black moods where any attempt at intervention would make him worse. He would also suffer night terrors of screaming while not being awake and would not remember them in the morning. He was extremely anxious and needed full adult attention in everything he did. He could not amuse himself without needing frequent adult approval.

NOTE:

You see from the above how the differences from his peers are being laid out and his social, emotional and communication difficulties are being shown to be a long-lasting problem. It is important to go into some personal background like this. It is after all, primarily a parental submission.

EXTRACT 4:

❝ Child A started at School 3 in September 2002. He made a few friends and was invited to tea a few times. He had already started to read and write before he started school but before long, he needed a **behavioural chart** because he was so stubborn and uncompromising. He always needed to be first or he would become distressed and cry or sulk, he couldn't sit still at carpet time and if upset would go and sit under a table. He found it difficult to work with other children and always needed to have his own way, becoming argumentative and tearful if challenged...

NOTE:

The first behavioural intervention in reception has been mentioned and put in bold so it is not missed by anyone who may, perhaps, be skim reading.

EXTRACT 5:

❝ **In Year Two** Time after time we were called in to speak to the teachers about his behaviour, how he would not follow instructions correctly, how his over-enthusiasm in PE would put himself and other children at risk and how his oppositional attitude made him difficult to teach. In addition, once he had been reprimanded by a teacher, he would sulk for the rest of the day. We decided that these social problems had continued for long enough and Child A's self-esteem was being seriously damaged, so we took him to see a paediatrician, "Doctor A". In his first Teacher Behavioural Checklist for "Doctor A", his teachers said that he upset other children easily, found it difficult to take turns or share, was often distracted, was easily annoyed and lost his temper very frequently, was often angry or resentful, argued with adults and interrupted others. [Encl: 1a].

NOTE:

So, here, we are building a picture of Child A's needs and the realisation that a medical opinion is needed. Enc: 1a refers to where the evidence for the assertion can be located in the submission.

EXTRACT 6:

❛ The infant school filled out Connor's Scores for Child A that showed he was highly **oppositional and impulsive, with few friends and upset others easily.** "Doctor A" said Child A was at the centre of a Venn diagram of classic autism, Asperger's Syndrome and ADHD, showing traits of all three. We tried him firstly on an exclusion 'Feingold' diet with some results. Child A stuck to the diet well, though in retrospect this was not surprising as he felt he was getting complete adult attention, which satisfied a huge need in him. He was later diagnosed, with Asperger's Syndrome with Hyperactivity, exacerbated by food intolerance. [Encl: 2]

NOTE:

This shows that the parents were taking measures to try to help their son, following doctor's advice. The child now has a diagnosis, upon which the case is based.

EXTRACT 7:

❛   By this time, Child A had moved up to School 1 Junior where we hoped for a fresh start. However, his first teacher questionnaire for "Doctor A" by his year three teacher (evidence attached) found that the same problems: failing to give close attention to schoolwork, impulsiveness, an 'obsessive' need to be first, excessive talking and shouting out, sulking, being physical with other children, continued to be evidenced. His teacher stated in the questionnaire that it affected his ability to make peer relationships and impacted on his learning and that he had definite social and emotional problems. [Appendix 1b]

IEP January 2006: *"Child A still has a need to be the first to finish and this reduces greatly the quality of his work"* This is also mentioned in his latest school report from School 2 , proof that this has been a continuing problem for a prolonged period of time. [Encl: 3a]

NOTE:

Here the submission quotes directly from the child's IEP, showing that despite his potential, his problems are having a detrimental effect on his schoolwork. This is important to show a direct correlation between the child's problems and how it affects school outcomes. The IEP will be submitted also by the school's SENCo but you want YOUR interpretation to be heard.

EXTRACT 8:

❛   In fact, it has recently come to our attention after we obtained a copy of the Appendix B submitted by Mrs D , SENCo at School 1 that it is clear they were well aware of Child A's problems and everything in Mrs D 's submission backs up our case. Although Child A was not getting the level of support that he is currently getting at School 2 , Mrs D states *"Child A was on SA on the special needs register but he did receive quite a lot of support targeting his behavioural and social difficulties. Child A would be taken out for 1:1 or in a small group. This support probably amounted to about two hours a week plus some in class support, depending on incidents that had occurred." [Encl 6]*

This indicates that Child A was already getting support at School Action Plus level in everything but name. It further strengthens our case that as this level of support had not had the desired impact over time, he should now be statutorily assessed.

Mrs D notes: "Child A's behavioural issues in class were as a result of his ADHD & ASD. He displayed behaviours typical of a child with these disorders and often these behaviours would spill out into the playground or football field. He became upset easily when things changed or didn't go quite as he expected them to... At times this inability to manage situations resulted in him being physical."

NOTE:

This is also key evidence, showing that the SENCo from the child's school believed him to require help far in excess the SEN level he was at. [The family then moved the child to another school, a private special school, School 2. They obtained further evidence from that school that strongly backed their case.]

~~~

Child A's parents felt they needed to engage the assistance of an independent Educational Psychologist to further strengthen their case. Sometimes you can convince the SENCo to call in the LEA Ed Psych for an assessment before you apply for your statutory assessment.

EXTRACT 9:

❛ Her (The independent Ed Psych) report did, indeed, find that Child A, while an extremely intelligent boy, has significant issues related to his rigid ASD thinking that will cause him considerable problems as he progresses through school. His scores show that while his verbal reasoning is at the 98th percentile, showing a good grasp of verbal comprehension, his non-verbal reasoning, showing the ability to understand and analyse visual information and solve problems was significantly much lower. His Working Memory and Visual/Motor Coordination skills were lower still, reflecting and explaining the difficulty Child A has in remembering class instructions, already described in this document. It also details how, because of Child A's "impetuous" style meant that he could work with speed when the memory load was comfortable but his, *"failure to employ a rehearsal strategy meant that he struggled with digits in reverse order or when the letters/numbers list became too long".*

The report says, *"This may be seen in class as a difficulty in remembering complex instructions or when he is not sufficiently motivated to give proper attention to commands. Child A may need to learn strategies...as learning materials increase in complexity."*

"Poor handwriting control, lack of mental flexibility and the tendency to become anxious under stressful conditions were all observed in the Coding task (and seen in the classroom if he is hurried or unengaged)."

Child A's Verbal Reasoning Score was on the 98th percentile but his Working Memory score was on the 61st percentile. While the latter figure is in the 'average' range it does not match the rest of his cognitive profile and, as Mrs F says, the profile is so uneven that the individual scores must be taken in isolation and not rounded together to make a general IQ score. It is not a case of "well he's doing better than most other children". A child like Child A cannot be compared to other children; these results show a great individual potential being undermined by his ASD difficulties. They can, however, be tackled with constant input in a specialised environment. Mrs F observed:

"At a technical level, the difference between Child A's Verbal Comprehension Index and his three other scores with this material meets with statistical significance. Such unevenness can often make learning a frustrating experience."

The report notes that, *"Child A has been diagnosed as fitting the ASD Spectrum and as such will have social* and emotional needs that will require **specific expertise and management in all settings."**

Mrs F concludes, importantly that: *"A statement of specific needs to be reviewed on an annual basis is relevant. Child A will thrive best in a small school, small class environment where staff have expertise in the area of social, communication and interpersonal skills development."*

We are simply asking for a Statutory Assessment so that consideration can be given about the necessity of providing a statement for Child A.

NOTE:

The report was enclosed in its entirely with the submission. I have only included a heavily shortened extract from that which the parents included in their submission. I believe it is important to highlight the areas of any reports you have within your own submission so that it is not overlooked by the SEN Panel that is deciding whether to assess.

EXTRACT 10:

" We would love Child A to attend a mainstream school for which we are already paying through taxes, but his welfare is paramount. We would love the county to be able to provide the kind of school Child A needs, but it does not. So we are left with no option but to ensure he gets his needs met through out of county provision, at School 2, which can provide everything necessary for him to succeed.

Our case is that Child A's needs are complex, pervasive and underlying and it would be virtually impossible for him to be supported adequately in mainstream secondary and certainly not unless his needs were statutorily assessed.

The following excerpt from recent research spells out the difficulties that particularly affect Child A:

"There is often an assumption that because a pupil with an ASD is academically able, he or she should be able to cope in mainstream school (Moore, 2007). However, as demonstrated in the current research, difficulties in social communication and interaction experienced by such pupils are likely to increase their exposure and vulnerability to bullying and social isolation (NAS, 2006; Whitney et al., 1994). Furthermore, the preference for routine, predictability and low sensory stimulation expressed by individuals with ASDs is at odds with the noisy, bustling and chaotic environment of secondary mainstream schools (Moore, 2007; Wing, 2007). Also, the typical cognitive profile and preferred learning styles of such pupils challenge professional assumptions about teaching and learning more than other groups of learners (Jordan, 2005). The lack of research and subsequent knowledge transfer in this area (in comparison to other SEN: Davis et al., 2004; Humphrey and Parkinson, 2006) unfortunately means that many schools are inadequately equipped to meet their needs: as Howlin states, 'our knowledge of how to help this

particular group effectively lags far behind' (1998, p. 317).

Humphrey & Lewis `Make me normal': The views and experiences of pupils on the autistic spectrum in mainstream secondary schools 2008.

The LEA must consider the following: Child A was offered a place at School 2 because they recognised the level of his social and communication needs hampered his learning. If Child A's needs were not severe enough then:

- Why would he have been offered a place at a special needs school and

- Why would we have sent an extremely bright child to a school for children with learning difficulties? If we had wanted to educate him privately, why would we not have chosen a regular prep school unless his needs were such that it was agreed he needed specialist schooling?

We are not seeking a so-called 'Rolls Royce' education, we are seeking a suitable education. We are not asking for more than that which any child deserves; the opportunity to make the best of his potential, which, according to the government, is what every child has a right to.

NOTE:

This is to answer any accusation that the parents simply want the LEA to pay for the private education of their child. The Humphrey & Lewis quote appeared in the journal "Autism" and was used as it is particularly relevant to Child A's case, as it may be to yours.

Using the LEA's own criteria:

The parents then went on to take the LEA's own 'Graduated Response' SEN document, read the criteria for statutory assessment for ASD children and show that their child fulfilled each criteria. For brevity, only a couple are included here as an illustration:

EXTRACT 11:

LEA Stated Criteria: "The child has difficulty participating within whole class group for significant part of school day despite SA+ arrangements. Curriculum access restricted. Greater curriculum emphasis required to address social and communication needs."

Parental Comment: In mainstream Child A was often upset and needed to be calmed by staff, which did not always happen in an appropriate manner for his condition (i.e., punishment rather than counselling). He was not able to understand how to work in a group (even in Year Four) and for example in ICT, would often work by himself rather than as part of a pair. This is because he had difficulty with turn-taking or taking account of the fact that others were not as able as him on a computer and he had a low tolerance level. The teacher would let him have a computer to himself because it was less trouble than to teach him the skills he needed to work with others and she was, understandably, very busy. He also needed to be taken out of class to attend special small group sessions for social and communication skills. Curriculum access was restricted because his working memory problems meant he did not understand or retain instructions and would rush through work because of his obsessive need to be first which had a detrimental effect on the quality of his output.

Mrs D, School 1's SENCo noted in her Appendix B: *"Child A was a very able boy but found it difficult to conform to mainstream expectations. He found working alongside others in a classroom difficult as he was often very focused on himself and 'couldn't wait' or accept that others had needs. He lacked the motivation to improve on his initial drafts and found change distressing. His ADHD meant he was often impulsive, causing mistakes but he found these difficult to accept."*

She also stated: *"Child A was a very able boy, however, his ASD & ADHD made it very difficult for him to function at the level of his ability... He had a rather idiosyncratic approach to learning, often becoming frustrated when attempts were made to change or modify his strategies and learning methods."*

NOTE:

The parental comment directly addresses the criteria with anecdotal evidence, backed up by a quote from evidence forwarded by School 1's SENCo.

LEA Stated Criteria: "Severely impaired social

communication skills requiring either intensive programme of social communication training and generalisation. Adaptation of communication by adults essential, with cues such as visual prompts and signalled routines."

Parental Comment: As above, Child A has been receiving some sort of social skills training since reception age when he had his first behavioural chart, but nothing has brought his skills up to the level of a 'normal' child. At School 2, where (where all children receive 'statement level' help,) he is finally progressing. In mainstream, signals were used in Y3 to help him realise when he needed to calm down and he was allowed, during Y4, to take a time out, but the nature of his problems means that social skills training needs to be intensive, sustained and on a daily basis as part of his educational experience. This he now gets at School 2 but is simply not possible in mainstream, certainly not without a statement.

NOTE:

Again, the criteria is used to show that Child A does, indeed fulfil the requirements for statutory assessment.

Further general points:

The application then makes wider points relating to the LEA and its published statements about SEN provision. These were researched on Google.

EXTRACT 12:

'   I would also draw your attention to the County Council Update on Reviews of Need and Provision under the SEN Development Plan 1998 – 2003 and The Required Capital Regeneration Programme 1.3 "Where pupil achievement or need indicates that mainstream schools are not appropriate and beneficial then specialist provision will be used."

The information submitted with this application points to a mainstream school indeed being inappropriate and indicating that specialist provision should be used.

The County Council's reply to the National Autistic Society's Make School Make Sense Campaign earlier last stated: *"The County Council currently maintains statements where children's major need is described as autistic spectrum disorders."*

I am making an assumption that the LEA would not have said this unless it was the truth, in which case Child A, whose major need is clearly described as an autistic spectrum disorder, with its associated difficulties, should have a statutory assessment so that consideration can be given for a statement. This response also admits that *"A lack of the county's own provision has led to the use of expensive non-County Council provision in some cases."*

The LEA, to my knowledge, has **no** provision of its own for children with complex, yet high functioning, Asperger's Syndrome who are not suitable for a specialist ASD school but who do not function well in mainstream school.

Included with this document are copies of Child A's IEPs and letters from his Paediatrician. You will see from the appointment on 10 December 2007, that Doctor A *said "the school is clearly meeting his needs very effectively"* and believes that School 2 is the right environment for Child A and the marked change he saw himself in Child A at a regular consultation since starting at the school. Doctor A clearly feels that Child A's needs are best met at School 2 and because of this, no longer needs to see him. This is stark proof that mainstream school was not suitable for Child A and at the very least, a detailed statutory assessment should be carried out by the LEA. [Encl 16].

Clause 7:35 of the Code of Practice states *"In considering whether a statutory assessment is necessary, LEAs should pay particular attention to:....evidence of the rate and style of the child's progress and evidence that where some progress has been made, it has only been as the result of much additional effort and instruction at a sustained level not usually commensurate with provision through Action Plus."*

If it was difficult for Child A's needs to be understood and met in a primary school, how, without a thorough assessment of his needs, will it be possible for them to be met in a busy mainstream secondary school?

NOTE:

You can see how each piece of research is used to underline the validity of Child A's case. You can research your own LEA's statements regarding special needs via Google or another search engine.

Finishing the application:

The application now moves into its final phase. Bear in mind these are only extracts and the full application is much longer—for Child A it ran to twenty-six pages.

EXTRACT 13:

' **What we believe Child A needs**

As his parents, we know Child A best. For Child A to achieve his potential and become a well-rounded functioning adult we believe he needs access to the following:

- To be taught consistently by teachers who understand the challenges that Asperger's Syndrome present to a child's learning.

- To be taught in small classes so that he is not disturbed by too much noise, meeting his sensory difficulties.

- To receive regular social skills training delivered in a way on a daily basis, within the classroom setting that he can understand and accept, to enable him to develop life skills and follow instructions rationally and objectively.

- Additionally, help to follow advice without assuming

he has failed; to increase his resilience to adverse events; to help to control his impulse to interrupt and call out; to help him curb his overriding need to be first which affects the quality of his work. This requires staff who have the time and training to deliver consistent help.

- To have his working memory deficits understood and supported so that he is not left 'to get on with it' because it is thought he is bright enough to manage.

- To have close contact with an adult mentor who understands him and can guide him, and to whom he can turn for advice when in difficulty or is upset to enable him to keep things in perspective. This is key to alleviating Child A's day-to-day feelings of anger and frustration at common events that he cannot make sense of.

- To be taught by teachers who can support his high intelligence and keep him consistently on task and motivated to want to achieve his best.

- To receive occupational therapy for his clumsiness associated with AS.

- To receive on-going Speech and Language Therapy to help develop his thinking and reasoning skills which often let him down and can lead to confrontation in difficult situations. SLT also to help ease his rigid thought processes which affect his learning.

- To receive support to improve his difficult left-handed writing style.

- To receive support to help to learn to work cooperatively with others; to take turns and to react appropriately to adverse situations.

Child A's education needs to be delivered in a specialist environment in small groups by teachers well-versed in the needs of high-functioning ASD children. Too often, children like these are left to 'cope' as best they can in the hope that they will somehow absorb social skills and resolve learning deficits by osmosis. The net result is that children such as Child A end up as underachieving and often troubled adults, unable to take their full place in society, often depending on social welfare or the already stretched mental health system. As parents, we do the best we can, but we need support from the education system to enable us to provide Child A with the level of support he needs to enable him to take advantage of life's opportunities in the same way as his 'normal' peers.

Clause 7:54 of the Code of Practice says *"In considering evidence as to whether or not it is necessary to carry out a statutory assessment LEAs should bear in mind the particular requirements of the individual child, and whether these requirements can be met from the resources already available to mainstream maintained schools and settings in their area in the context of school-based intervention, monitoring and review arrangements."*

In conclusion, I believe we have proven without doubt that Child A is at the very least in need of a detailed statutory assessment so that his needs can be thoroughly assessed. His needs are so complex and difficult to understand at a daily teaching level that it impossible for them to be met without an in-depth investigation into how his difficulties can be addressed. We know he has enormous potential and that with the right teachers and environment he can overcome his difficulties but we fear that unless his needs are fully understood and the provision to ensure they are met spelt out, in mainstream he would have no chance of achieving his academic or social potential.

~~~

The application then listed the evidence used, numbered to correspond with the references within the application.

The content of your document will likely be very different from the above, but you can see from the way it is laid out and the language it uses that it is speaking to the professionals on their terms, while getting across everything that needs to be said as parents. If you find this approach too daunting, feel free to set it out as you choose, but ensure that you refer to your key pieces of evidence. Feel free also to use whatever wording from this document that fits your child.

This is your opportunity to relate your parental opinion and your experiences of your child's difficult behaviour and underachievement but do your best to make sure that your opinion is backed up as much as possible by professional evidence. You must speak from the heart but you can't expect the Special Needs Panel just to take your word for it if you don't have the evidence from schools and/or educational and medical professionals to back it up.

The Special Needs panel are looking for hard facts that are impossible to ignore. They are making decisions that not only affect your child but also affect their budget. If there is room for doubt, it will be seized upon.

They have to judge who, on the continuum of need, should be assessed – a process which in itself, costs money. Allowing an assessment is one step closer to spending big money on support so you need to be convincing that your child needs one. LEAs, especially these days, have diminishing budgets and an increasing number of parents wanting their child to have a share of it. Someone's going to miss out – make sure it's not your child.

A second, brief example

Child A, above, is a very unusual young man in his educational profile. It has been used in such detail above to show you how to construct your argument, and the kinds of evidence you might wish to use. It touched slightly on the use of percentiles, which for a child who is significantly underachieving will be much more crucial.

Below is a short extract using Wechsler Scores:

EXTRACT CHILD B:

'   The **Wechsler scores** show a great discrepancy between Child B's Reading and Numerical operations. His reading of single words was on the 5th percentile, with spelling on the 7th. Meanwhile, his basic number skills were at the 50th percentile. This is evidence that, far from being incapable or just naturally not very bright, Child B's lack of success in reading and spelling is in stark contrast to his numerical ability where he is performing at a level comparable to his age.

It is true, everyone has strengths and weaknesses, **but to be working at three to four years behind where you should be is a huge cause for concern**. This alone should be reason enough for a statutory assessment. But when you couple this with Child B's uneven profile should trigger action.

Added to this, **his Working Memory was at the 2nd percentile** which indicates that even if he has a chance of understanding instructions, he cannot hold them in his head long enough to do anything useful with them. This means that not only does he have great difficulty with reading, he finds it difficult to retain the information that he *has* read. His processing speed, however is now said to be average, and this, coupled with his Working Memory problems and inability to hold onto auditory instructions, leads to frustration for him. It is noted that his processing speed may well have improved by now being in the correct educational environment and receiving OT and SLT.

In this area of Working Memory, the report found that his scores have dropped in relation to his peer group since his October 2005 Dyslexia Assessment and this is despite being at a specialist school. Imagine how this would be if he was in a 'regular' school environment.

NOTE:

Wechsler Scores are provided by an Educational Psychologist. If you can get your SENCo to organise an LEA Ed Psych assessment of your child before you apply for a statutory assessment you will have these at your disposal. Otherwise you will need to arrange for a private Educational Psychologist. You can find one near you via the internet or from recommendation. Bear in mind, they are very busy and there may be a wait before your child can be seen. You may need to pay their travel fees if they are to visit your child at school.

Expect to pay upwards of £500.

A Third Example

In this case, the parents used the headings provided by the LEA to help them organise and present their case but ensured that they also included evidence. I have used a selection of the LEA headings and brief extracts from the parents' submission. I have also added notes to help point out areas of specific interest.

A. My Child's Early Years

Health:

Child C was born by emergency caesarean at 32 weeks old, as I (his mother) had pre-eclampsia. He was immediately taken the Special Care Unit where he suffered complications. Thankfully he recovered but was hospitalised for a total of seven weeks as he struggled to maintain his blood oxygen levels.

At the age of five, it was determined that Child C only had one kidney. He is diagnosed as having chronic kidney disease stage three. He had to be admitted to various hospitals ten times between the ages of 5 and 6. He now unfortunately, but understandably, has an on-going needle phobia. It should be pointed out that throughout all of these investigations; Child C found it all very difficult to cope with. He was incredibly anxious whenever we crossed the threshold of any hospital. It was a very worrying and disruptive time.

NOTE:

A child's physical health background is relevant, as it can have affected his ability to learn.

Education:

For his first year in school, Child C set himself apart from his peers both physically – by not playing and joining in, and mentally he was way behind in reading, letter phonics, and maths. He was not disruptive or ever a problem, but he was happier if he was left to play on his own – which is what the teachers did. At the end of this school year, he was held back for a second year to accommodate him and the over thirty class size.

It seemed that Child C already showed signs of being different, something that he was very aware of and he felt very excluded watching the friends that he had spent the last year with move to a new classroom, with a new teacher. We were never made aware of any concerns or suggestions that Child C had any Special Education Needs.

When Year 2 arrived Child C found it very hard to re-join his original year group, both socially and educationally. He had missed out on building friendships, and had leapt from an environment based around play, to one where emphasis was on learning with play almost restricted to break times. He naturally found it very hard to adapt and in fact from almost the first day in this year group he did not want to go into school. Nearly every day it was a challenge to get him through the door, and every day he cried and so did I.

As he progressed through the school to the end of Year Three it became more evident that Child C was really struggling to 'keep up'. At this point we were informed that Child C was on School Action, which we were told meant that he would have 'a little extra help' in a small group with other children that were behind in maths and literacy, with the class Learning Support Teacher.

Child C's school life changed dramatically when I attended a Parents Evening when Child C was eight. His teacher said "Child C is the most frustrating child I have ever taught", and continued for twenty minutes describing him as lazy, having a very poor concentration span etc. etc. I commented that this report was the same as every report he had ever had in his life and asked what we could do next. I suggested that there was obviously something wrong with him and what help could they offer. Both teachers had no idea and referred me to the Head teacher.

I refer to the LEA's Inclusion Policy:

Effective inclusive practice is based on two core values:
Equality - all children should be equally valued regardless of their abilities, circumstances or behaviour. Education enables people to develop respect and responsibility for themselves and others. Action needs to be taken against discrimination.

I fail to see how the aforementioned teachers have complied with this Policy. Indeed, I find it incredible that these teachers were not even aware that Child C had Special Education Needs and had been placed on School Action within this school!

Having heard the buzz word 'statement' I met with the head teacher. She told me that they could not help me with any assessments or statements and that I would have to employ the services of a private assessment, and once they had a copy they would see what help they could provide – but of course budgets were tight and they could not offer any additional support to Child C unless instructed to by the LEA, which would bring with it the relevant funding.

Not once was I offered any guidance. In fact through my research for this document I have found the County Council's leaflet –'What are Special Education Needs' and paid particular notice to the following reference:

The Code describes how help for children with special educational needs in early education settings and schools should be made through a step-by-step or 'graduated approach'. At an early stage you should receive information about the local Parent Partnership Service.

How I wish the teachers, SENCo and Headmistress had been made aware of the support available to parents like me. Undoubtedly, it would have avoided my husband and I pulling Child C out of this mainstream school.

NOTE:

The parents submitted reports from the schools to

back up their claims of educational underachievement. Their experiences with the school not being willing to help the parents with the statementing process is, sadly, one that is repeated all too often. Here they are also quoting from the LEA's own literature.

We then appointed an Independent Education Psychologist to carry out an Educational Assessment of Child C. (Appendix 2). At her request the school carried out a Performance Record assessment (Appendix 3) and concluded that Child C was performing below average levels in all of reading, writing, spelling, comprehension, speaking/listening, maths, science, geography and languages. And his NFER results in May 2006 gave him the spelling age 6:05 and reading 6:06 – two years behind his average peers.

The Ed psych said if Einstein is 100 and you and I are fifty, Child C is three. She suggested that he have an Occupation Therapy Assessment and have his eyesight checked. We employed the services of a private Occupational Therapist (Appendix 4). This information may well have helped the teachers but we felt there was very little help offered to us, to carry out support and help at home.

The report showed that Child C's Perceptual Reasoning was only at the 3rd percentile – borderline and his working memory, processing speed and full scale results were all low average. The percentile ranking and qualitative descriptions, together with the following statement, left us in no doubt that Primary School could not provide the suggested support, and at the very least he should be on School Action Plus if not already statemented.

NOTE:

This was a key piece of evidence showing that Child C was significantly behind his peers and had difficulties that were preventing him from learning.

Physical Skill:

Child C has always preferred the outdoors, and over the years we have observed that he is able to enjoy and engage in any activity that has a practical application, and these activities are usually individual sports. However, he really struggles with team games such as football, rugby and cricket although he likes them he finds it almost impossible to deal with the ball and what he should be doing with the rest of the team.

Hand writing was one of the first signs of problems when he was six. It has improved immensely since taking drugs for ADHD. Previously he just wanted to get written the bare minimum so that the task was done – it seemed as though he had no pride in his work. The same if he were ever asked to colour something in – he would always just use one colour randomly covering the page with colour.

Playing and learning in the home:

As you know Child C was diagnosed as suffering with ADHD, in August of this year. Having this diagnosis has helped us as parents by allowing us to research the condition, understand him more, and be able to manage him better within the home environment.

We have never seen Child C use his imagination at play, in fact as a younger child he would never play with cars, trains, action figures and still doesn't. He has never been able to join in with board games, construction kits such as Lego, Meccano etc., obviously due to his lack of concentration. I have always likened Child C to a 'pinball ' – he flits from one thing to another – TV, computer, PlayStation, playing outside etc., and none of the activities captivate him for longer than a maximum of ten minutes.

He openly gets angry and frustrated at most things and can regularly be heard as saying "I can't do it" or "this stupid thing", and when someone offers to help he gets increasingly angry and storms off, as though he has given up.

NOTE:

The parents got a solid diagnosis for their child, which has helped in realising what help he needed.

General Views:

From the history provided in this contribution it is clear that we, as Child C's parents, have worked really hard to ensure that Child C's health and welfare needs are met in the best way possible. We have provided evidence to show that we have always sought the best help for him as was possible in each situation.

The educational journey has been more of a roller coaster ride, for us all, but the path that has finally led to Child C being in the best possible environment must have been damaging and disruptive to Child C, especially to a child that finds new environments particularly daunting. If we had been given the support and guidance that should have been offered, through his Primary LE schools, his needs may well have been met in his initial mainstream school, causing minimal disruption. But it was not.

There obviously has been a huge cost implication to us through funding the recruitment of external agencies that through private assessments of Child C, have given us the answers we have needed to determine his problems and provide the right solutions. Had the LEA provided the much needed guidance and support as promised in SEN Policy, through its schools, perhaps there would have been a different outcome, and we certainly would have been financially better off as a result.

So we are certain that we have done everything possible to get to this point. One would hope that this statementing request would acknowledge our efforts, and also acknowledge the lack of support that Child C has had a right to.

NOTE:

The parents clearly demonstrated that they have worked hard to find solutions for their son before resorting to beginning the statementing process.

After this submission, Child C was assessed and statemented. However, the LEA recommended a school that the parents knew could not support their son. After a battle, during which they hired the services of an SEN lawyer, the school backed down and agreed to pay fees for the independent special school where Child C is now thriving.

It all seems too much...

So you've read everything above and it all just seems too complicated.

Don't be disheartened.

The examples provided are designed to help you organise your thoughts. If you make notes as you go through your evidence you will be able to break things down into useable chunks. Some of what is written above may be relevant to your child, if so, please do use it.

What might be useful is to write your story first and then underline areas where you might be able to find evidence from your documentation – such as medical letters or school reports. Then look through those reports to pick out paragraphs that support your case. Insert the quotes from the letters/reports into the right spot in your application and note where it is from. Leave any numbering of enclosures until the end.

It is also just as valid to organise your application by using any headings the LEA have provided for you. This may help with organising your thoughts and setting it out. Just remember to include your evidence.

If you have supporting evidence such as a Speech Therapy report, there is nothing to stop you producing a "Parent's Comment on the Speech Therapy Report", stating why you agree or disagree with specific ideas.

Another idea is to include a report of "Everything we as parents have tried, to help our child". It shows that the school have tried and you have tried, but your joint efforts haven't worked and you are now desperate for the right support.

The point of this book is to ensure that you don't sell yourself short by not providing sufficient evidence with your application. The point to using quotes from your reports is to highlight the areas YOU think are important and not leave it up to the Special Needs Panel to dig them out of the many documents you may have provided. The point to commenting yourself on the excerpts you use is to ensure that they draw the same conclusions as you!

What now? – The painful wait

After you are satisfied that you have done a complete job on your application and have, with trepidation, sent it in (send it recorded delivery at the very least) you have the unenviable task of waiting.

Keep a copy for yourself and keep the originals of all your reports – only send the LEA copies. Keep a record too of any and all communication with the LEA and your case officer, even telephone calls. Make notes of phone calls so that you can refer back to them later.

A word to the wise: The LEA is not obligated to provide "the best" school for your child, merely one that can meet his needs. There is suspicion in LEAs that parents are just trying to get the LEA to pay for expensive independent placements. If you are aiming for an independent school after you have secured a statement, you need to prove that the LEA does not have a school of its own that can meet your child's needs. You will see this illustrated later in this book.

Use this time to research schools, if you haven't already. With our boys, we had already moved them to the school of our choice. However, I still researched the local comprehensives and special schools so that I could make a case that these establishments were not suitable for my boys. I rang up the SENCo for one school that had an ASD unit. She said to me, "Well, we often don't see them for months at a time, until something goes wrong." What? They're left without emotional support until the proverbial hits the fan? I thought. I don't think so, not for my son!

I also visited the SENCo of the local comprehensive who knew exactly why we were there. She knew we had no intention of sending our son to her school if we could help it. She was in complete agreement that our son was in the right school already and although she didn't say it, I was pretty sure that she would support us when we said they couldn't support his needs at their school.

What I was doing, was getting my ducks in a row for that small window of opportunity (currently 15 days) when, if we got the statement, we would be able to send in our preference for a school.

When you visit the schools, prepare a set of questions aimed at your own child's difficulties and likely needs. This way you can ask the same questions of each school and take notes. Write a report on each school, so that you get a clear picture of whether they can/can't meet your child's needs. Use these visits and reports to work out which is the best school for your child and to back up your request for a specific school.

The LEA has a specific period of time to consider your application. If they haven't got back to you by the end of it, start to hassle them. They will usually wait until the very last minute. Get to know your case officer and try to establish a rapport with them. This may not be possible, some are impossible to get hold of, but try, at the very least.

We've been turned down!

The letter arrives and it's bad news. The powers that be have decided that your child's needs are not severe or complex enough to warrant a statutory assessment. You will be devastated, angry and upset. But do not despair or give up. Take a day or so to vent your fury and mull over whether you want to fight on.

If you do want to continue, you can appeal to SEND, the Tribunal that hears disputes between parents and the LEA. You can easily find them on the internet and their processes and forms are all available for download.

You might, at this juncture if you haven't already, want to seek help from one of the wonderful charities such as SOS!SEN, IPSEA or, if your child is has an ASD, the National Autistic Society's Advocacy Service. You can find the web addresses for these at the Special Needs Jungle website or by searching on Google.

We were turned down initially when we applied for each of our sons. The first time, it turned out they had missed out several crucial documents. This was discovered by our case officer, with whom I had fostered a good working relationship. She arranged for the case to be sent back to the panel and they tried to fob off the missing reports as irrelevant. Not long after I registered my appeal with SEND, they changed their minds and decided to assess.

The second time, for my older son, I happened to go to an SEN workshop where the new Head of SEN for our county was speaking. She spoke of high-functioning children with Asperger's whose needs it was difficult to meet and who needed to be given the right support. She also mentioned that they wanted to cut the number of appeals being registered against them.

Heart pounding, I went up to her afterwards and told her about my son, whom she could have been describing in her speech, and who they had just turned down for assessment.

She told me to send her the application documents directly and she would look at them again. I agreed to hold off on my appeal until then. I have no idea what went on behind the scenes of the LEA but the refusal to assess was overturned within a very short space of time.

It's not likely you'll be blessed with the same piece of luck as I was if you are turned down, but it shows that you need to keep your wits about you, get informed and don't be afraid of seizing any opportunity that comes your way to make your case.

Appealing

If you decide to appeal, you will need to download the forms from SENDIST or apply for their informative pack which will give you lots of information. If you want to and can afford it, you might like to seek the advice of a lawyer at this point but be warned, if you lawyer up, so will the LEA – they may anyway. If you can't afford it or do not want to go down this path but feel you need support, I strongly advise that you contact one of the charities already mentioned. Their help can be invaluable.

There are so many horror stories about the antics and tactics of LEAs at Tribunal and because of this I would urge you to seek advice as mentioned, if only for moral support.

You will need to gather every document that you sent in for your original application. Did you have an Ed Psych assessment done? If not, maybe you could consider one but as you have a limited amount of time to get your documents in, you will need to hurry.

Keep the lines of communication open with your case officer, if possible. If new evidence comes to light – a report you have suddenly got hold of for example that may tip the balance, it is worth approaching them for a change of heart. It is possible!

I've quite often heard of cases where the LEA didn't bother to turn up to Tribunal or back down the day before your case is due to be heard, after you have gone to the trouble of getting witnesses, childcare, days off work, not to mention the hours spent .

Bear in mind you have a set amount of time to register your appeal, currently, two months. This is two months from the date you receive your refusal letter from the LEA. You will need to send a copy of this letter with your appeal.

You will need to convince the Tribunal that the school could do no more to help your child with the resources it has. If the Tribunal decides the school could do more at the current level of help, you will lose your appeal. This is why you need to get a list of all the interventions the school has already tried with little success.

IPSEA have a very useful "How to appeal" pack that is available for free download from their excellent website. There are also useful guidelines for setting out your appeal on the SOS!SEN site.

If you get a lawyer, they may advise you not to speak to the LEA at all. That's up to you – if you can get a reversal of decision before a tribunal, isn't that surely preferable? The Tribunal says that even after appeal you should continue to try to sort out the matter with your LEA. This is important advice. If you can show that you have made every effort to get the LEA to re-look at the case, including offering to meet with the Head of SEN and still they are refusing to give a reasonable response or respond at all, then this will weigh against them at Tribunal.

If you have done a thorough job of preparing your initial application you will already have all the information you need to send to the Tribunal. Bear in mind the Tribunal are less interested in your child's background and more interested in their needs today, so you may want to amend some of your original application for assessment document accordingly if it contains a lot of background.

You will need to fill in the form you have been sent or have downloaded from the SEND website, stating your reasons for appeal. Send it along with your LEA decision letter, your (amended) parental submission stating why your child needs an assessment and all your evidence to the tribunal within the two month deadline. Remember, only send copies, not original documents

Once the LEA has received notice of your appeal from SEND they then have 32 working days to respond saying whether or not they oppose your appeal. Appeals are expensive for LEAs and they may choose, once they know you have appealed, to look again at your case.

If they choose to oppose your appeal they have to defend their position, supplying reasons why they have taken that decision. If they don't respond at all they may be barred from taking any further part in the proceedings.

The road to Tribunal

If the LEA decides to fight your appeal you should most definitely seek support or advice as already suggested if you have still not done so. They have a wealth of experience in going to Tribunal. Or, you may wish at this point to consult a specialist SEN lawyer. This option however can end up costing thousands of pounds.

Once your appeal is registered, the Tribunal will send you information about deadlines for further information, if you have any, and when you need to let them know about witnesses.

Your SENCo may be reluctant to be a witness, especially if their evidence will support your case. They will be worried it might get them into trouble with the LEA. At least one LEA has told its schools, staff and Special Needs Co-ordinators (SENCos) that they must not volunteer to support parents at an SEN Tribunal, citing parents who have an "agenda" to send their child to an independent special school at the LEA's expense. If a witness refuses to come, the Tribunal can issue a summons but you need to write to the Tribunal in enough time saying why it is important that the witness attends.

~~~

It is important to be aware of the process of a Tribunal and what you will be faced with. Julie Maynard is a parent of a special needs child and a long-time SEN campaigner and advocate. She has helped many parents through Tribunal and there are few people who can explain the procedure better from a parent's perspective. Here is her viewpoint:

_____

The Tribunal, by Julie Maynard

Sitting at a hospital waiting to see a Consultant Paediatrician, many months after my son Joshua's birth, I reflected on his traumatic start in life. He had been premature, needing intensive care in a special baby unit. I remembered only too well the days sitting by his incubator, looking at him on a ventilator, fighting for his very existence. But that was all behind us now. Sadly, I was wrong. Joshua's premature birth was to come back with a vengeance.

Leaving hospital, having been informed Joshua had cerebral palsy, my dreams of how his life would be, came crashing down around me. Little did I realise, that I was about to undertake a journey to arrive at a place I never knew even existed. A place I did not know how to get to, or for that matter wanted to go to. I also did not appreciate just how rocky the road would be. But somehow, by hook and by crook, with the aid of the Internet, the help of charities and the guidance of wonderful parents who had been there, I finally arrived at my destination, SENDiST.

When Joshua was diagnosed I had not appreciated I needed to ask my Authority to undertake a statutory assessment of him. This was to ensure he would receive extra help in his mainstream classroom or attend a special school. He was under a range of health and educational professionals through his nursery placement, but not one person mentioned the magic words – 'Joshua requires a statement of special educational needs'.

I was only to discover this simple reality because the nursery school Joshua was attending was being closed. When I sought advice from charities, I was suddenly informed of Joshua's entitlement to help. I did not know if I was angry for being so naïve, or hurt that the professionals there to help Joshua hid this very fact from me, a fact upon which my son's educational future and progress would depend. And such parents do need to seek advice, as believe me, authorities rarely choose to advertise their services.

I requested the Authority to undertake a statutory assessment of Joshua when he was three years old. It refused on the grounds it was too early – thus pre-judging the outcome to see if Joshua required a statement or not. I immediately appealed to SENDiST. I was an able articulate parent, who was not going to be thwarted. I researched thoroughly, looking for ways to build up my evidence. I obtained private assessments of Joshua, referrals for second opinions through the NHS and support charities. I was so glad I did; Joshua, in addition to his cerebral palsy was diagnosed with an autistic spectrum disorder. A few weeks before the hearing, the authority reversed its decision, agreeing to assess Joshua. When Joshua's statement of special educational needs was issued, I was compelled to appeal to SENDiST again.

During this time, other parents approached me asking me if I could represent them in Tribunal. I agreed. I have now been doing so for the last thirteen years. I found I was able to detach myself from the child I was advocating for, without muddling an emotional response to the facts about a child's special educational needs. Accordingly, I unwisely thought I could do the same for my son. I was spectacularly wrong. I lost my Tribunal because my judgment and reasoning were clouded by my personal feelings and knowledge of Joshua. As it transpired, the Tribunal erred in law. The High Court subsequently set aside the decision, and ordered a new hearing. I did not make the same mistake again. I appointed a barrister to represent me at the new hearing.

Most of the parents I represent feel the information sent by SENDiST via a DVD does not equate to the reality of the actual hearing. It seems evident to them that what the DVD portrays, as an informal process, comparable to a genteel game of Sunday cricket for amateurs, is simply untrue. Sadly, the reality in my opinion is that SENDiST is often a bruising Saturday afternoon professional rugby game. Without a good referee, namely a representative, things in the hearing can get very rough indeed.

Parents need to understand that SENDiST is governed by legislation, regulations and complex High Court rulings known as English case law, which most parents struggle with. The hearing itself is only as informal as it can be under such rigid circumstances. That said, all hearings are different and not comparable. The hearing is conducted in front of three people, namely a judge and two panel members who have expertise in the field of special educational needs. Often they are conducted in a way that suits the personality of the panel members, their personal approach, view and sometimes prejudices to the evidence; and most importantly of all, the judge's management of the hearing. Just like in criminal and civil courts, some judges in SENDiST are more experienced and better than others.

Further, some local authorities will appoint barristers, others will have very experienced SEN officers. Both parties are entitled to bring three witnesses. The Tribunal does permit more if an application is made but only in exceptional circumstances. It is therefore important for parents to seriously reflect who they wish to be witnesses, asking the question what educational knowledge of the child does the witness have to assist the Tribunal in its decision making process. Parents and the authority can ask for an observer, prior to the hearing or on the day itself. The Tribunal can agree or refuse, even if the authority has no objections.

The hearing takes most of the day. It can be adjourned for another day, if not fully heard. Prior to the hearing a numbered bundle is produced by Tribunal, and sent to both parties; parents must ensure all their witnesses have their own copy of the bundle at the hearing, the Tribunal can become cross if witnesses do not have bundles or have to share them. It is important for parents when raising a point to direct the Tribunal to the pages in the bundle they rely upon.

Parents may ask questions of the Authority's witnesses, but not usually its representative. The panel will ask pointed questions on the basis of the written evidence each party has submitted in advance of the hearing. Parents are then invited to present their case, with the Authority being given the opportunity to question them. It is because of the numbered bundle that the Tribunal can and is reluctant to accept new evidence, especially on the day, and will only consider doing so if a formal application is made. If a parent intends to bring new evidence it must produce five copies and provide it to the authority prior to an application being made.

The hearing can be an emotional roller coaster, especially as the authority is given the first opportunity to present its case. It may wrongly seem to a parent that they are not receiving a fair hearing at that stage. It is therefore important not to panic at this point, but to remain focused. Taking notes of what the authority's witnesses say is important, as their evidence does need to be summarised at the end of the hearing in what is called "summing up". The parents have the final say. It is important to ask for a brief adjournment at the end of the hearing to prepare for the 'summing up' process, in which parents should summarise clearly the evidence the Tribunal has heard, and why the Tribunal should place more weight on it, than that of the evidence of authority.

The Tribunal at the hearing is not interested in the events of the past, it merely contains itself to what are the identified special educational needs of the child now and how are those needs appropriately met. It will not involve itself in parents' perception of alleged wrongdoing by a local authority in the past.

The Tribunal does not like parents or witnesses talking over each other or interrupting. Sometimes, it is hard to remain quiet when something is said, but nonetheless, a Tribunal will warn both parents and Authorities regarding its conduct in the hearing. It is important to keep as calm as possible.

It is not for parents to demonstrate an authority's proposals are unsuitable; it is for the authority to persuade the Tribunal that its proposals can meet the child's need. It is important to gather evidence that correctly identifies the child's needs and what support they require to access the curriculum. Finally, I personally would always urge a parent to appoint a representative or ask a charity to assist them both prior to the hearing and at the hearing itself.

Once the hearing is finished, parents have to wait fourteen days for the decision.

A parent's response to the decision if they win, is often not elation, but a sense of relief, followed by feeling angry. But remember, once an appeal is over, a parent will have to continue to work with the authority regarding their child. If a parent adopts a sense of bitterness, it will not help build bridges in the future.

And if you lose your decision? Seek advice as soon as you can from a charity or representative. SENDiST does make mistakes. If it has erred in law, as it did in my own child's case, then you may be able to appeal against it. Finally, parents should not be daunted by the Tribunal process or hearing. Things will be fine providing they have sought proper advice and guidance. Good Luck.

We're being assessed!

Well done you! The LEA now has a set amount of time to carry out an assessment. This will include, almost certainly, an assessment by the LEA Educational Psychologist. You will also need to meet with the psychologist after the assessment of your child as they will also want to speak to you to gather your impressions. Make sure you think ahead of time what you want to say – make notes if you need to. This is your chance to speak to a key influencer in the decision of whether or not your child gets a statement.

The Ed Psych should have reviewed all the documentation you have already submitted and they will carry out a number of standardised tests on your child. They will also speak to your child at length.

If you have any other information that you have not already submitted, such as reports you have only just got hold of, send it in during this time. You want your case to be a strong as possible.

If you haven't already researched schools, do it now. You won't have time if you get a statement to start from scratch.

There may be other assessments such as Occupational Therapy or Speech and Language unless you have already had recent reports already to hand. My younger son had had all these already as well as an assessment by an ASD Outreach worker. His Ed Psych assessment came 18 months after his first one by the same LEA Ed Psych who reported that his numerical skills had actually deteriorated in that time!

After the assessment(s) you will again be playing a waiting game. Again the LEA will wait as long as possible – often to the day of the deadline.

When the letter finally comes, it will be a day of happiness or despair. Either way, your job is not yet done. If the news is bad, again you must decide whether to push on and appeal through the SEND Tribunal, hopefully using the same help as already mentioned. You could give up at this point and decide that the LEA must be right, and you have nothing left in you to fight. Or you could believe that you've come this far and the wrong decision has been made and you will fight on to get what your child needs. This is, for everyone in this position, is a difficult decision that is not taken lightly

If, however, you letter brings good news, you still have work to do before the process if finished. If this is your outcome after your application, you will now have fifteen days to state your preference for a school. If you have researched them already as suggested earlier, you will have a good idea of which school you want.

You've got the statement, now what?

The proposed statement is set out in six key parts.

- **Part One:** This is your child's general information and all the information the LEA received as part of the assessment.

- **Part Two:** This is where all your child's needs, as assessed by the LEA is set out. Read this carefully to ensure that it matched your own view of your child's SEN.

- **Part Three:** This is where the provision the LEA will provide to meet those needs is set out. This needs to be gone through carefully as it rarely measures up to the promise of part one.

- **Part Four:** Names the school that your child should attend. Once the final draft is agreed and a suitable school is named, the LEA is also responsible for transporting your child to and from that school. This should be left blank by the LEA in the proposed document but often isn't!

- **Part Five:** This describes any non-educational need your child may have. Ensure that and Speech and Language Therapy or Occupational Therapy is included in Parts Two and Three as these have been proved to be educational needs.

- **Part Six:** This final part describes who will provide the support to meet the non-educational needs described in part five.

~~~

As mentioned, you now have fifteen days to make the case for the school you want. If you are lucky, the LEA will concur with your choice. If, however you want an out of county placement or an independent specialist school, you will have to convince the LEA that this is the best way to spend their money.

This is also your opportunity to ensure that the statement measures up to your child's needs and I have found that this is rarely the case. You need to analyse each point in Part Two of the draft statement that you will have received and ensure that it matches up with the provision that has been set out in Part Three. Part Four is the naming of the school the LEA wants for your child.

The LEA has a duty to ensure that provision is clearly specified as to what will be provided, for how long and by whom. Go through your draft statement with a fine toothcomb to ensure that this has been done. All too often the provision is not spelt out and is worded in a vague way. Each identified need MUST be met with clearly stated provision.

In both my sons' draft statements stated need was often met with no provision at all. The way the document is laid out makes this difficult to ascertain. It does not say here is the need and this is what we're going to do and how. It has part two with all the needs, then part three with all the provision.

It is up to you to check through this. Make a table with headings of 'Need' 'Provision' and 'My comments'. Then take each need and put it in its own row in your table under column one, 'Need'.

Next, search through Part through to find a provision that might match. If and when you do, enter this into column two next to the need. Now see if what has been suggested is clear and specified. If not, make your notes about this next to it in the 'My comments' column.

If the need is not met with specific provision in each case, the document is breaking the law. Point this out in your response.

~~~

Below is the placement document from Child A so you can see how this can be done. It is quite lengthy, but some of the points made may help you if you come across similar points in your own draft statement and it will help you understand how to deconstruct the statement to ensure that the final statement adequately reflects your child's needs and required provision.

~

Parental Response to Proposed Statement of Special Education Needs for Child A

We are very pleased that the LEA has decided to statement Child A. However, it is our view that placing him in a mainstream secondary, specifically our local secondary, even with 18 hours support, would be extremely detrimental to his education and to his emotional state.

We have taken the time to visit the school and its SENCo, and while she clearly does an excellent job and it is a good school, we do not believe Child A would thrive in a large secondary and it is not the right environment for him.

The following document explains in detail, highlighting from reports that should have already been seen by the panel and analysing the proposed statement, why we believe the LEA should name School 2 as the appropriate placement in Part Four of the final statement.

Because of the way the proposed statement is presented, I have tried to create a table below that marries up Part Two, needs, with Part Three, provision. In some cases the two have been matched quite well, in others there is no provision at all and in yet others it is difficult to see how Child A's needs can be met in an environment that is so unsuited to him.

NOTE:

*To reiterate what I said earlier: Start with Part Two and split up each separate stated need (as stated by the LEA) into separate sections. Then, go to part three and try to match up a need with a stated provision and ensure it is specific. Finally, make a note of any of your own comments. You might find it useful to do this in a three-column table. Call column one: **Part Two – Special Educational Needs.** Call column two: Part Three – **LEA Provision.** Then call column three:*

86

Comments

For easier layout within the book, I have set these out illustrating several of Child A's points for illustrative purposes...

1. Part Two – LEA stated needs: Behavioural Emotional & Social development-: Child A" is fiercely competitive to the point of always wanting to be first and finding it hard to cope with failure; He is driven by his own agenda and if not interested in a particular topic can find it hard to engage; Child A tends to be confrontational and easily loses his temper, reacting with physical or verbal aggression;

Part Three – LEA proposed provision: Child A will have access to teaching assistant time to help him build and maintain social relationships through individual and small group social skills work including looking at friendships, working cooperatively, taking turns and reacting appropriately to situations. This will include practical guidance and problem solving, individual support with anger management and emotional skills. He will need help to transfer those skills to the classroom.

Parental Comments: To take the last point first, how will he be helped to transfer 'skills' into the classroom? The way to transfer them is to teach them in the classroom in the first place, as happens at School 2. At School 2, Child A has made friends and it is imperative for his future self-esteem and learning that these friendships be allowed to develop.

2. **Part Two – LEA stated needs:** He has a strong sense of right and wrong and lacks flexibility of

thought. However he is much better at listening to and accepting advice now and usually makes an effort to put it into practice.

Part Three – LEA proposed provision: Nothing mentioned

Parental Comments: This point shows that his "needs" are being well met at School 2, there is nothing to offer in mainstream and there is no moral reason to move him for the sake of two thousand pounds a year. (see cost analysis later)

3. **Part Two – LEA stated needs:** Child A is highly sensitive and easily becomes anxious.

Part Three – LEA proposed provision: Nothing provided

Parental Comments: This is a major problem. How can his sensitivity and anxiety be managed and minimised in a large Secondary school where he will feel lost and alienated?

4. **Part Two - LEA stated SEN:** Child A interprets remarks and situations of difficulty very much with himself in the centre and often feels blamed and disliked when others comment.

Part Three – LEA proposed provision: Child A needs to learn ways to adopt a more varied perspective on events. He needs to be taught strategies which children normally 'pick up' through life experiences some of which he is unlikely to intuitively grasp but needs practical strategies and methods.

Parental Comments: How will this be delivered alongside a busy academic curriculum? At School 2, this is delivered a part of his everyday timetable because of the way the lessons are delivered. He is not withdrawn from lessons at School 2.

Additionally:

LEA proposal: Staffing: Within a mainstream setting, Child A will have access to teaching assistant time for 18 hours per week for small individual, paired and small group intervention, working under the guidance of the teacher/SENCo to:

- Implement emotional and behavioural development strategies, including a trusted adult

- Implement social skills programme and support his social skills in social situations.

- Support his learning and access to the curriculum

- Support fine motor and handwriting skills development.

Parental Comment: My main issue with this is that because of the nature of Child A's needs, the help he needs is of a continual 'nudge' rather than sitting with a teaching assistant to overtly learn 'social skills'. This has been tried before at School 1 without much success. At School 2, this kind of work is incorporated into every lesson as most students need this kind of help. The proposed statement says Child A needs 18 hours support a week, but my concern is that he would be withdrawn into small groupings during academic lesson time. This would be counter-productive to his learning whereas at School 2, his academic learning and is social learning are integrated within lessons.

Child A will have a transition plan for Secondary Transfer"... This is now too late to implement as his Y6 school finishes in one month.

Child A currently receives Speech and Language Therapy at School 2 and there is nothing in the proposed statement that acknowledges this as a need and there is no provision for it. This is a vital part of Child A's therapy at School 2.

Furthermore, Child A is happy at School 2. He has finally made good friends and the fact that this is no longer a stress for him means he is more settled and supported in lessons by his peers. The children at School 2 are not like those in a regular mainstream school. They have all 'been through the mill' themselves, and are more willing to make allowances and to support their peers. It is in large part because of this that Child A has progressed as he has. To move him to a large secondary school would seriously jeopardise this work and if it is only to save the difference between £12000 at School 2 and £9000 in mainstream, then this has to be seen as a negligible financial differential.

NOTE:

The cost analysis is important, especially if your request is turned down and you find yourself heading for a SEND Tribunal. The Tribunal does not take too kindly to LEA's trying to save a couple of thousand pounds when the needs of the child are clearly better served by the slightly more expensive school.

Cost analysis for LEA proposed school as named in Part Four –

Approx. Cost of Local comprehensive 2007/08:

£3506

Current SA+ Funding=   £1081

Current Eight hours (above 10points) 423x8=

£3384

MINIMUM TOTAL= £7971

This figure does not take into account any additional capitation costs per statemented pupil and so is more likely to be around the £9000 mark. If we compare this to the cost of School 2 for the current year at around £12000, I am sure the SEND tribunal would see the difference as being negligible compared to the benefit to the child.

NOTE:

This information was all sourced from the internet using careful search terms. If it's just not there, ring up the schools in question or ask the LEA itself to provide a cost for their recommended school. If the differential is considerable between the school you want and the one they want your child to go to, you will need to work hard at proving that your preferred school is the only suitable option for your child.

Section 9 of the 1996 Act requires local authorities and the tribunal to have regard:-"to the general principle that children are to be educated in accordance with the wishes of their parents, so far as that is compatible with … the avoidance of unreasonable public expenditure"

Recent rulings however may mean that this detailed breakdown of a maintained school place will not work as well if the differential is high. In B v Worcestershire County Council [2010] UK UTA 292 (AAC), Judge Williams said, "Disproportional precision is not necessary. Rather it is a balancing exercise in which the probable comparable costs of the two placements are part. What is required is sufficient accurate information to ensure that everything material to the final decision is considered in that balancing exercise. ..."

Part Four of the proposed statement

Part Four of the proposed statement is where you wish the placement to be. The LEA may name their own choice of school here, which is not that likely to be the one you want. It is a good idea to approach the school you want before this time to ensure that they can offer your child a place and support their needs. Get this in writing so you can forward it with your amendments to the proposed statement.

Child A's parents worded their response to part four as below. Again, this is only an extract.

Parental Response to Part Four

We have reviewed all the evidence that was submitted during Child A's statementing process and it

is impossible to find a single professional who met him that would recommend placing Child A in a mainstream secondary with or without support – even the LEA's own Educational Psychologist. There is, however, plenty of evidence that recommends placement in small, well-structured classes, being taught by professionals who, as well as the required subject knowledge, also have insight into the learning styles and needs of children on the ASD spectrum. To ignore such overwhelming advice would be foolish in the extreme and not something we would accept. I repeat here the relevant sections of the submissions for Child A's statement to back up our contention:

NOTE:

The submission then reiterated points from the evidence that supported their assertions. It then goes on to state:

EXTRACT: The LEA does not have any schools in its control which can provide a suitable environment for high-functioning children with Asperger's Syndrome. This is already acknowledged by the Head of SEN, It is also a fact that the LEA fund many children at School 2, including our younger son and so there is direct precedent for placing Child A there at the LEA's expense.

Please note that we have **no intention of claiming for transport** for Child A if he were to be funded at School 2 by the LEA, even though we live more than three miles away from the school.

You should also know that if the LEA does not name School 2 in part 4 of the statement, we will appeal to SEND without hesitation. We are immovably determined that Child A should remain at School 2 and we are convinced that it would be the best possible use of LEA resources to fund his place there. It is our belief that if we do so, with the evidence that we have presented and from studying previous cases at Tribunal, that the relatively modest cost of School 2 coupled with a lack of suitable provision within the county, will lead the Tribunal to find in our favour. We have avoided appealing in this case so far, where the needs of Child A have been agreed to be clear and we would hope that common sense will prevail. **Therefore we wish Part Four of Child A's final statement to name School 2**.

NOTE:

The cost of providing transport for statemented pupils is a massive headache for LEAs, coming in at millions of pounds a year. Sometimes, transport is necessary to get the child to the school because of the distances involved and the circumstances of the parent. In this case, saying they would not be claiming for transport was used as an additional carrot, followed by the threat of the stick, that having come this far, there was no way the family would back down now on getting the right school. In this case, it worked and the placement was made for School 2.

As a point of interest, if the family wanted to claim for transport at a later date, they would still be able to do so. This is because that once the LEA names a school in Part Four and only that school, they then become legally responsible for getting the child to that school.

Note, you only have fifteen days to make your comments on the proposed statement. If your placement request is turned down and you have to appeal, ensure you appeal parts 2, 3 & 4, using your analysis of the stated needs and provision as detailed above. Again, if you need help use the charities that are there to support you.

~~~

If, after this journey, you end up with a placement at the school you want for your child and the support you need, you should congratulate yourself. You have worked hard on your child's behalf and given them the best chance of success in later life.

You may have encountered stumbling blocks along the way and you may have needed to spend money you can ill afford on reports and appointments. You may have had help from various sources or you may have gone it alone. The process is likely to have caused tears of frustration, confrontations or family disruption.

But it is the end result that matters.

Parent Views

Below are a few views from parents on what they had to go through to get their child the help they needed:

Pam said:

"When I requested an assessment for a statement, I told my son's life story, which was also my story for the previous ten years. I tried to make sure that I had included everything, however insignificant; I wasn't put off by the very small space on the form. Because there had been a lot of negative experiences both for my son and for me concerning my son, it took a lot out of me to get it all into print. When I had finished and read it all through, I didn't feel relief; I felt a lot of pain because there was no place left for denial. There were many sad tears at this stage. Unfortunately once I was caught up in the "statementing process", there were quite a few more tears but these were tears of frustration and anger. Naively I had assumed that the role of SEN was to find the best solution for each child but actually their role is to avoid acknowledging a child's needs and if they can't avoid acknowledging them, to avoid quantifying them so that there is no way for parents to insist that their child's needs are actually being met. It is an ordeal and I honestly don't know how the people who work for SEN sleep at night.

However I found it in myself to fight my corner because as determined as SEN were, I was more determined because I wasn't fighting for myself or for the local authority budget, I was fighting for my son.

When the LEA agreed to assess, they requested assessments from all their equivalent professionals. I spoke to my SEN officer at the LEA and found out the names and addresses of the LEA professionals. I then contacted the speech therapy department and found out what reports had been sent to them about my son. They had received only the speech therapy report, so I immediately sent out (by recorded post) my full submission, including all reports to each of the professionals appointed to assess him.

The immediate effect of this was that I had a phone call from Speech Therapy to say that they would have to cancel my son's original appointment and re-make that appointment with a senior speech therapist, because it was obvious that he had complex needs. I know that the LEA professionals sometimes say one thing to the parent and then write another in their report, but I was very, very fortunate, because I got a lot of sympathy from the people assessing Jed. I think they felt my pain before they even met me or began assessing my son.

I think it is a really good idea to produce this guide because honestly I just sort of fumbled my way through the process, but a lot of people wouldn't be able to cope with that. I was powered by desperation and fuelled on by people telling me that my child wouldn't get a statement. To me the statement was the only way to get help for my son, so as mentally exhausting as it was, I just kept going. I didn't want to give the LEA any excuse to put off their decision so I made sure I covered every angle. After bereavement going through the process of applying for and getting a statement is the most stressful experience I have ever had. Divorce and moving house aren't even on the same page."

~

Kima said:

"My son is not statemented, but I believe a couple of useful things came from our efforts to do so. We put an application into the catchment state school where his brother goes. We were offered a place. I arranged a meeting there as no one else was going to find out what they could do for him.

The meeting was attended by the head Ed Psych for the LEA, someone form the LEA Education Department, the Deputy Head and a Special Needs Coordinator. My husband and I prepared questions designed to find out what assistance he might get. The answer apparently was none, despite the Ed Psych suggesting all sorts of strategies, the Deputy Head said they couldn't meet his needs. Clearly she wasn't supposed to say this as they are funded to assist students with special needs. We thought she was being refreshingly honest!

As a result it sparked an investigation at the school and Hants saying they would assess him for a statement. While he was being assessed, the person from the Education Department came to our home and without asking us, had gone to another school and came to tell us they could do everything he needed. Very clever move as now they could say he had been offered suitable state provision, so no need to statement him or fund a place at the school we actually wanted. We would never send him to the school she suggested as we had removed our eldest son, who is very bright with no difficulties as he had such a bad time there.

But according to the education advocate we consulted that meant they had fulfilled their duty. He was refused the statement. So my advice would be to seek a meeting at a state school and grill them hard about what they can do without a statement. As well as not letting the Education Department find another school without your knowledge of where they are going first."

~

Lin said:

"One big problem for me was organisation, my filing was poor and I needed to have stuff to hand from years ago, all the medical and psychiatric reports had to be found.

Good record keeping will save many frustrating hours. It is good to log phone calls and get things in written form where possible. If you are organised you will be better able to tell when dates are coming up and so and be ready to chase people frequently. The biggest problem is always that authorities are often not helpful and are more likely to obstruct the provision of suitable care on the grounds of cost, as they control the decisions on placement and budget. I'm having a second son statemented now, so we'll see about that.

I had a lot of help from the NAS education helpline with my application, they went through it thoroughly with me, they are great actually."

~

Clare said:

"Paper work, evidence and expert reports are a must. I gave up my college work to place my son first as I am dyslexic and couldn't do both to the best of my ability, so my son without doubt came first. I spent many hours on the PC until the early hours of the morning writing letters, emails and copying everyone into this paper work, which included the educational lawyer, the doctor, my son's specialist and social services (social services didn't want to know, as they told me I did not ill-treat my child). There were also others who were included too. It took over my life, though when the Tribunal date arrived, I was at the Tribunal to WIN! And win I did, I won transport and even a laptop. I included all sorts of evidence, as much as I could get, and followed every letter up when the LEA ignored me, so have ever since sent all letters to the LEA by recorded delivery, for they cannot be trusted! Ignoring people is the LEA's most powerful weapon, though this never intimidates me now! Intimidated is what they want you to feel, so you will go away! I did not go away!

Our case notes were near on one thousand pages, which included much thought and concentration from a dyslexic mother. I'm sure it was the two-and-a-half year battle which made me ill with my ME and Fibromyalgia, though would I have changed a thing? Absolutely not! My son is so worth the struggle. I had to get him the appropriate education he so desperately needed."

~

Michelle said:

"We didn't get to tribunal in the end. We came to an agreement that I said I would be willing to do the transport if the council paid for his education and boarding. However, a year after another boy in my son's year at the same school achieved the funding with transport. He is only two miles from where we live! The departments who make up the authorities don't speak to one another! However, it's worth asking authorities, for emergencies sake, if there is a pick-up in your area. This is the difference in what direction you go to seek help. I had a consultant who supported me who knows much about dyslexia and court proceedings, we didn't use a lawyer but you're not guaranteed the outcome you wish however you tackle it. The direction we went in was very time consuming. You are organising the meetings to obtain the reports you need, driving to meetings and photocopying A LOT as I had to send of a huge amount of paperwork to four parties concerned. You have to be on the ball. It's an anxious time. It makes you feel ill to say the least. Time is precious. It helps, if you run your own business from home, or don't go to work, so time is flexible."

101

Fiona said:

Local authorities in England know of around 20,000 home-educated children. When Ofsted surveyed a small number of home educated children in 2010 it asked to meet with home educating families and Ofsted inspectors reported that over a quarter of the 130 home educated children they met had special needs, with many on the autistic spectrum and though we cannot generalise from a small self-selected sample, my experience as a volunteer for a home education support charity does suggest that unmet special needs is a recurring reason for parents opting for home education. Problems with schools' not meeting their children's needs had finally prompted these parents to take their children out of school.

In a number of cases the children had also been bullied or desperately lonely and miserable at school and sometimes this was the deciding factor in choosing home education, with parents frequently saying they felt they had no choice.

Once parents take their children out of school for home education, they find that many forms of support are reduced or stopped and the only consistent contact parents have with the local authority is at the Annual Review of the statement of special needs.

The law says that parents are responsible for their child's education, either by sending them to school "or otherwise" and in England or Wales when a child has a statement of special needs, the parents don't need to ask anyone's permission before they start home educating unless the child is registered at a special school. For more information, of elective home education see http://edyourself.org/

~

Emma said:

Our son was diagnosed with classic autism at three. At that stage, his problems with language, social interaction, anxiety, academic delay and physical co-ordination were so severe that our paediatrician thought he would go straight into a special school for children with autism. Having fought for, and got him some excellent support over the years, he is now an engaging 13 year-old (with the usual teenage attitude!) with a wide group of friend, is accessing a modified version of the curriculum for his age and is expected to take GCSEs.

Once we'd got over the initial shock of diagnosis, I went into research mode and started gathering all the information I could about how we could best support him. I tracked down every acquaintance or colleague whom I knew had experience of the world of special needs, bought them a coffee and mined information from their heads.

The thing I wish I hadn't done was to just put 'autism' into a search engine - there are some awful stories out there which I found of limited use and terribly depressing. Absolutely everything I read or heard indicated that early intervention was very beneficial so I had a sense of urgency, as I knew that if we could get some support in place before he started school, he stood a better chance of benefitting from the education system. I found out pretty quickly that this sense of urgency was not shared by the Local Education Authority! I found out the name of our case officer (cases are allocated alphabetically by surname, so it's not too hard to do) and wrote to him in December 2001 asking for our son to be formally assessed for a statement. The reply came back four weeks later saying that our son had not been notified to the LEA by a local health authority (different to our authority) and that "it is usually best if a request for a formal assessment is made after a child has commenced school for a period of time so that the LEA can obtain more information and a clearer view of the child's present and future needs". Ha! I thought, stuff that!

So I then found a sample letter showing me how to formally request assessment, invoking the Education Act, and attaching evidence in the form of his diagnosis, an SLT report, details of a review with the paediatrician and a home visit report from the autism school outreach. My lever arch file was filling up! I also found out that the LEA had in fact been informed about our son's diagnosis four months before, but that this was the first of many items which had 'gone astray'.

Two months later, I received acknowledgement that our son would be assessed, but with a caveat that this may not lead to a statement. This was now March, seven months after diagnosis, and our son was due to start school that September. As a summer-born child with global delay, it was clear he wasn't remotely ready for school, so we put in a request for him to stay on at nursery, requesting a place at a special needs nursery and were told in the March that he could be 'considered' for this placement.

By the end of May, nothing had happened, and I was getting no response from our case officer, so we wrote requesting a meeting to try to find out what was happening. The meeting was a farce, but nonetheless, despite the statement still not being complete, he was awarded a place at a fantastic special needs nursery with one to one support and speech therapy on tap.

A year later, the transition to a special needs unit in a primary school was relatively straightforward as I had a better understanding of the process and managed it like a military campaign (I was now on lever arch file no.3). However, we had a few stressful days after a friend who was going through the same process with a different case officer had had a phone call saying that her son had a place at their chosen special school, but we had heard nothing. I eventually got hold of our case officer, who was pretty cross that I had phoned him and grudgingly said that we had a place at the school our choice. He said that reason that my friend had heard about their placement was that they were at the beginning of the alphabet and we were at the end!

Our son's statement was then maintained every year until his year 4 review, when an Educational Psychologist who had never met our son before announced that, as he was out of year, he would have to move to senior school at the end of year five, missing year 6 completely. We therefore started another appeal, initially for him to stay on at his junior school until the end of year 6, but later changing this to a request for him to go to a specialist independent language and communication school. At this stage, we employed (very expensive) solicitors who advised us to obtain independent assessments and reports from a speech and language therapist, an occupational therapist and a psychologist. They recommended which specialists to use as they said these were the people in our area who knew best how to write reports to help succeed at Tribunal.

The solicitor also said that his statement was in fact illegal, as although we had letters saying it was maintained, it had never been updated when he moved from nursery to school. There was much to-ing and fro-ing between us and our LEA over a year, with them in turn suggesting that our son should indeed stay on at his junior school (but then start senior school in year 8, thus missing all the settling in process); go to a moderate learning disability school (he is of average IQ) or attend the local secondary school, which has virtually no special needs expertise and which, according to the very helpful SENCO, could not possibly cater for a child with needs as complex as our son's.

Just six weeks before we were due to go to tribunal, and almost eighteen months after we had first lodged our appeal, we had a meeting with our barrister who suggested that, as we were able to take our son to school ourselves, we should offer our LEA a 'trade' whereby we would forego transport in exchange for the place at the independent school of our choice. And two weeks later, on the last day of term, they accepted. It was the best Christmas present we have ever had.

Conclusion

I hope this book has given you a clear and useful explanation of how to go about writing your child's statutory assessment application and beyond. It is, in places, very detailed but this was necessary to demonstrate the type of information that may be needed to prove your child's case. Yours doesn't need to be as detailed as long as you have included your views and all the evidence but it is wise to make sure that key parts of your documentation are not overlooked by the panel.

You may find that the school is willing to apply for a statement on your behalf. If so, great, but make sure they have all the necessary information and external reports you may have had done. Don't be a bystander to your child's education.

You may have noticed two themes running throughout the book. Firstly, if in doubt that you can manage, get help. If you end up going to Tribunal, that goes double. Secondly, remember when you are low that you are doing this for your child and their future and hopefully, remembering that should give you the strength to keep going when things look difficult.

Do not underestimate the stress, anger and maybe even despair you will feel at times through this process. But remember, you're not alone. Even if your family and friends aren't much help, there are message boards and websites, such as mine that can help offer support.

At the end of the process, it is to be hoped that you will have secured what your child needs to ensure that he has the support he needs to access the curriculum and get the education he deserves. Remember, you're not asking for more than any 'normal' child gets on a daily basis—the chance to learn in a suitable, safe environment.

Please feel free to leave a comment on www.specialneedsjungle.co.uk or on the site where you bought it if you have found this book useful.

I wish you good luck.

References & Links

1. SEN Code of Practice. Downloadable from www.education.gov.uk
2. Humphrey & Lewis, Make Me Normal http://aut.sagepub.com/content/12/1/23.short
3. IPSEA http://www.ipsea.org.uk
4. SOS!SEN http://www.sossen.org.uk
5. NAS Advocacy:

    http://www.autism.org.uk/advocacy
6. SEND Tribunal:

    http://www.justice.gov.uk/guidance/courts-and-tribunals/tribunals/send/appeals/index.htm
7. The Education Act 1996:

    http://www.legislation.gov.uk/ukpga/1996/56/contents

Acknowledgements

Thanks for buying this book. I hope there are no errors but if there are, they are my own. Do let me know if you find any factual mistakes so they can be rectified.

Thanks must go to my husband, Marco and two wonderful sons, Luca and Giorgio. We have been through and are still on this journey together. I know that because of their fantastic school they now have a much better chance of achieving their ambitions.

Thanks also to the NAS Advocacy service, who gave support to me when I was preparing both my sons' applications. The NAS is a wonderful charity; please remember them when you're choosing a charity to donate to. Even buying Christmas cards from them helps.

A big thank you to Pam Szadowski for reading through the manuscript and making useful suggestions, to those parents who generously allowed me to use extracts from their applications and from those who contributed their viewpoints.

Thanks must go too to Maria Hutchings, a wonderful lady, for the foreword and to Julie Maynard for her incredibly valuable contribution and for sparing me so much time and enriching my SEN knowledge beyond my own experience and research.

Other books: Tania Tirraoro

Tania Tirraoro also writes women's fiction.

This Last Summer is a family drama, which also features a gifted young man with Asperger Syndrome.

Sweet Seduction is a simple, feel good, pure romance.

These books are available from major ebook retailers and in bookstores.

http://www.tirraoro.com – Author site

http://notasadvertised.blogsport.com – Tania's non-SEN Blog

Lightning Source UK Ltd.
Milton Keynes UK
UKOW050132111111

181852UK00001B/1/P